Edward Broughton Broughton-Rouse

The Law of Heriots

With an Introductory Note on their Origin

Edward Broughton Broughton-Rouse

The Law of Heriots
With an Introductory Note on their Origin

ISBN/EAN: 9783337233020

Printed in Europe, USA, Canada, Australia, Japan

Cover: Foto ©ninafisch / pixelio.de

More available books at **www.hansebooks.com**

The

Law of Heriots

WITH AN INTRODUCTORY NOTE ON
THEIR ORIGIN

BY

E. BROUGHTON BROUGHTON-ROUSE,

M.A., LL.M., Cantab.

———

PRICE FIVE SHILLINGS.

LONDON:
BUTTERWORTHS, 7, FLEET STREET,
Law Publishers to the Queen's most excellent Majesty.
1892.

[*Entered at Stationers' Hall.*]

Cambridge:

PRINTED BY J. WEBB & CO., ALEXANDRA STREET.

PROEM.

In placing before the Public this brochure on the Law of Heriots, I entertain little hopes of its ever finding many readers, for I am well aware that to most people—including members of the legal profession—the subject will appear dry and abstruse, and, from its small importance now-a-days, worthy of but little notice. But for me—the son of Rolla Rouse of the Middle Temple, in his day a leading Authority on Copyhold Law—this little-trodden bye-way of the Copyhold "Great North Road" has many attractions; and my attempt to render plain its ins and outs, and its many twists and turnings, I dedicate in all reverence to my Father's Memory.

E. B. B-R.

Cambridge.

CONTENTS.

AUTHORITIES REFERRED TO.

Bacon's Abridgment.
Best, Chief Justice.
Blackstone's Commentaries.
Bosworth's Anglo-Saxon Dictionary.
Bracton.
Britton.
Brooke's Abridgement.
Cases and Opinions [Pub. 1791].
Cnut's Secular Dooms.
Coke's Compleat Copyholder [1641].
Coke's Institutes.
Cruse's Digest.
Fitzherbert [La Graunde Abridgment].
Fleta.
Gilbert's Rents.
Gilbert's Tenures.
Jacob's Law Dictionary [1756].
Kitchen.
Liber Assisarum.
Lyndsey's " Monarche."
Maine's Early Law and Custom.
Plowden's Queries.
Rolle's Abridgement.
Scriven [by Brown].
Tacitus.
Thorpe's Diplomatorium Ævi Saxonici.
Viner's Abridgement.
Watkins' Copyholds.

REPORTS.

FULL TITLES OF REPORT.	PERIOD.	REFERRED TO AS
Adolphus, J. L., & Ellis, T. F.	1834—1840	A. & E.
Barnewell, R. V., & Cresswell, C.	1822—1830	Barn & Cres.
Bingham, P.	1822—1834	Bing.
Bosanquet, J. B., & Puller, C.	1796—1807	Bosanq. & Pull.
Brownlow, R., & Goldesborough, Jno.	1569—1624	Brownl.
Bulstrode	1609—1639	Buls.
Carter, Samuel	1664—1676	Carter
Cowper, H.	1774—1778	Cowp.
Croke, Sir Geo., Eliz		Cro. Eliz.
„ „ „ Jac. i.	1512—1641	Cro. Jac.
„ „ „ Car. i.		Cro. Car.
Douglas, S.	1778—1784	Dougl.
Dyer, Sir J.	1513—1582	Dy.
East, S. H.	1803—1812	East
Gale, C. J., & Davison, H.	1841—1843	Gale & Dav.
Godbolt, J.	1575—1638	Godb.
Hobart, Sir H.	1603—1613	Hob.
Hutton, Sir R.	1612—1639	Hutt.
Keble, J.	1661—1679	Keb.
Keilway	1496—1531	Keilw.
Law Reports	1865—	L.R.
Leonard, W.	1540—1615	Leon.
Lutwyche, Sir E.	1682—1704	Lutw.
March, J. (Brooke Trans.)	1515—1558	Mar. Bro.
„ (New Cases)	1639—1653	Mar.
Modern Reports, T. Leach	1660—1755	Mod.
Moore, Sir F.	1512—1621	Moore
Owen, T.	1556—1615	Ow.
Plowden, E.	1550—1580	Plow.
Salkeld, W.	1689—1712	Salk.
Saunders, Sir E.	1666—1673	Saund.
Shower, Sir B.	1678—1695	Show.
Vernon, T.	1681—1718	Vern.
Willes, Lord, C. J.	1737—1758	Willes
Wilson	1742—1774	Wils.

CASES QUOTED OR REFERRED TO.

The figure refer to pages.

Abingdon *v.* Lipscombe, 27.
Attree *v.* Scutt, 24, 27, 28, 29, 34.
Austin *v.* Bennet, 17, 18, 19.
Baldwin *v.* Noakes, 18.
Bruerton's case, 26, 27.
Butler *v.* Archer, 23, 24.
Chapman *v.* Pendleton, 27, 35.
———— *v.* Sharpe, 25.
Edmunds *v.* Moseley, 18.
Ever *v.* Aston, 26.
Garland *v.* Jekyll, 15, 24, 27, 28, 29, 34.
Gerrard's case, 25.
Griffen *v.* Blandford, 20.
Hix *v.* Gardiner, 17, 23.
Holloway *v.* Berkeley, 24, 27, 29.
Lanyon *v.* Carne, 19, 23.
Lemal *v.* Cara, 24.
Lloyd *v.* Winton, 18.
Major *v.* Brandwood, 17, 18, 19.
Norris *v.* Norris, 24.
Odiham *v.* Smith, 18, 21.
Osborne *v.* Steward, 19.
———— *v.* Sture, 18, 23.
Parker *v.* Combleford, 21, 23.
———— *v.* Gage, 17, 18.
Parkin *v.* Radcliff, 14, 18, 20.
Parton *v.* Mason, 21.
Polyblank *v.* Hawkins, 25.
Rowden *v.* Malster, 31.
Shaw *v.* Taylor, 20, 21.
Talbot's case, 27, 35.
Trin. Coll. Cam. *v.* Browne, 24.
Tyrer *v.* Littleton, 22.
Wilson *v.* Wise, 21.
Woodland *v.* Mantel, 18.
Zouche, Ld., *v.* Dalbiac, 36.

.

INTRODUCTION.

PROBABLY no incident of land tenure in England is of greater antiquity than the Heriot. The word itself is doubtless derived from the Anglo-Saxon "here" an army and "geatu" or "geatwe" preparation, apparel, adornment—though Lord Coke gives an alternative derivation from the Latin, "herus dominus," because it was appropriated to the lord.[1] The heriot is often regarded as an institution of Cnut, but there are many examples of the custom in the Charters much earlier, which show that he simply declared the law of an ancient—probably primitive—usage. Considered now as but an obscure accompaniment of copyhold tenure, the heriot a thousand years ago was a very important thing indeed. In those days its payment was frequently equivalent to the handing over of all a tenant's belongings. Ten centuries since a man's most valued possessions—often his only possessions—were his arms of offence and defence, and his other accoutrements of war, and these, on his death, passed, not to his children, but to his lord. The horse and weapons, which in the strict theory of the Comitatus had been the loan of the chief, had to be returned at the death of the vassal, in order, according to the same theory, that they might provide another henchman with the implements of service. And this seems not unnecessary in a country where the materials of which weapons are fabricated are not abundant, as was the case in England at that time, for iron was imported from Spain up to the fifteenth century. Tacitus notices the same fact as to the lack of iron in Germany, "ne ferrum quidem superest sicut ex genere telorum colligitur." In course of time the Heriot became limited to a portion only of the deceased's military belongings, for cap. 72 of the Secular Dooms of Cnut runs thus: "And let the heriots be as it is fitting to the degree, an eorl's such as thereto belongs that is

---

[1] Coke's Compleat Copyholder, 1641.

eight horses, four saddled and four unsaddled, and four helmets and four coats of mail, and eight spears and as many shields, and four swords and two hundred mancuses of gold.[1] And after that a king's thegn's, of those who are nearest to him ; four horses, two saddled and two unsaddled, and two swords and four spears, and as many shields and a helmet, and a coat of mail and fifty mancuses of gold.   And of the medial thegns a horse and his trappings, and his arms ; or his 'healsfang' in Wessex ; and in Mercia two pounds ; and in East Anglia two pounds.   And the heriot of a king's thegn among the Danes who has his soken four pounds and if he have further relation to the king, two horses, one saddled and the other unsaddled, and one sword and two spears, and two shields and fifty mancuses of gold ; and he who is of less means two pounds."[2]   Cap. 75 provides that the heriot shall not be demanded when the tenant dies in battle.   Some Saxon wills contain express bequests of a heriot to the lord, for instance that of Wolgith, A.D. 1046, and another dated circa 946[3] where the testator bequeaths to the king his heriots, viz: four swords and four spears, and four shields and four torques, four horses and two silver vessels.   At first sight these wills appear directly opposed to the notion that the heriot was claimed by the lord as a *right*, but there is great weight in Mr. Watkins' argument[4] that such wills were made only out of abundant caution that the testators might not appear unmindful of their lord, and to prevent the chattels of the deceased from passing into other hands and especially into those of the Church, and the expressions in the will of Wolgith appear to admit the lord's legal right.   Between 944 and 946 Æðelgyfn devised lands and chattels to St. Albans " cum consensu domini mei regis " and in the same century Beorhtric, a wealthy noble in Kent, devised land by will to various relatives. He left the king a collar worth eighty mancuses of gold and a sword of equal value, his heriot comprising four horses, two of which were saddled, two swords with their belts, two hawks and all his hounds.   He give to the queen a ring worth thirty

---

[1] The gold Mancus was worth about six shillings (Bosworth's A.S. Dictionary).
[2] Ancient Laws and Institutes of England, 1840.
[3] To be found in Thorpe's Diplomatorium Aevi Saxonici.
[4] Wat. Copyh. ii.

mancuses of gold and a mare, that she might be his advocate [forespræce] that the will might stand, "ðæt se cwide stondan mihte."[1] Many such wills being made and allowed to hold good, testators in course of time probably claimed as a right the power of leaving as they chose such of their belongings as were not strictly heriots, and what was at first scarcely a custom grew into a law. Blackstone was of opinion[2] that a heriot was originally a voluntary donation or gratuitous legacy of the tenant, perhaps in acknowledgement of his having been raised a degree above villenage when all his goods and chattels were quite at the mercy of the lord, but the heriot that Blackstone had in his mind was of course that of the ceorl or husbandman, not that of the eorl or theign—not the *military* heriot. Very shortly after the Conquest the custom arose of commuting the heriot in kind for a sum of money. Such was the custom in Normandy before the Conquest, and the payment of money was usual in the time of Henry the Second. In *Assisa de armis habend. in Angl.* 27 Hen. ii. we read, "Si quis hæc arma habens obierit, arma sua remaneant hæredi suo. Si vero hæres de tali ætate, non sit quod armis uti possit si opus fuerit, ille qui eum habebit in custodiâ, habeat similiter custodiam armorum et hominem inveniet qui armis uti possit in servitio domini regis si opus fuerit donec hæres de tali ætate sit quod arma portare possit et tunc ea habeat." Hence it is clear that by the twenty-seventh year of Henry the Second the lord had ceased to have any claim upon the military equipment of his tenant and that by that time a money payment must have been substituted for it. Although very early in the times of the Norman kings the Saxon heriot became confounded with the Norman relief yet as a fact the two differed essentially. The heriot has been generally a personal and reliefs always a predial service.[3] The word "relief" appears to be derived from "relevare" to lift or take up again. It is the sum paid by the heir to the lord on *taking* or *lifting up again* the inheritance of an estate which had as it were fallen to the ground by the death of the ancestor. Heriot is the act of the leaving, relief the act of

---

[1] Cod. Dipl. No. 492.
[2] Black. Comm. ii. 377.
[3] Jacob's Law Dictionary, 1756.

the incoming, tenant or heir. But the maxim that "there is no rule without an exception" would appear to be capable of application to heriots, for in the case of *Parkin* v. *Radcliffe*[1] it was shewn to be the custom in the Manor of Marsden for a heriot to be paid by an *incoming* tenant. Heriots appear to have been not unknown in Scotland, for Sir D. Lyndsey[2]— Scott's " Sir David Lindsay of the Mount, Lord Lyon King at Arms "—speaks of a " herield hors " meaning doubtless a horse yielded as a heriot. It seems then that the heriot in its inception was purely military, and consisted of the weapons and accoutrements of the tenant, which upon his death became vested in his Lord ;—that by the time of the Conquest a certain portion only of such weapons and accoutrements passed to the lord ;—and that soon after the Conquest it was compounded for by a money payment and became indistinguishable from the relief. Had it not become so confounded it must have fallen with the military tenures which were extinguished by the Act of Charles the Second.[3] Nevertheless the heriot has not perished utterly ; for, in analogy to the military heriot there arose the villein heriot, *i.e.*, the heriot of the villein, ceorl, or husband-man, either of some beast of agriculture or of some inanimate chattel, and this heriot survives to our day. The unfree settlers on a lord's land, who were not called upon by their tenure to perform military service, by their demise made payable to the lord their best chattel [*melius catallum, best head*, in German " beste haupt "]—heriot custom as opposed to heriot service— probably on the theoretical hypothesis that he, at the commencement of the tenancy, had supplied the necessary implements of agriculture. From the authorities it would certainly appear that this villein heriot was originally a gratuitous bequest of the tenant. Bracton, the author of the book called Fleta, and Britton [this last is by many considered to be but an abridged re-issue of Bracton], are all agreed as to this. But inasmuch as in very early times all the goods and chattels of a villein were the absolute property of his lord, the gratuitous nature of the heriot must have dated at the earliest from the

---

1 *Parkin* v. *Radcliffe*, 1 Bosanq. & Pull. 393.
2 The Monarche, Bk. iii. line 4734.
3 XII. Car. ii. cap. 24.

time when the villein had gained at any rate a qualified property is his goods. Chief Justice Best hazarded an opinion that the villein heriot might have originated in offerings made by an inferior to a superior when he approached him for any favour, or to be taken under his protection, in accordance with the custom that prevails even now among Eastern nations.[1] But be the origin of villein heriots what it may, only that species of heriot now exists, and it is divided into Heriot-custom and Heriot-service.[2]

---

[1] Judgement in *Garland* v. *Jekyll*, Bing. ii. p. 272.

[2] Devonshire leases for lives often reserve a money-payment on the death of each life as a "Farlieu." Bailey in his Dictionary says, "Farleu or Farley is a duty of sixpence paid to the Lord of the Manor of West Slapton in Devonshire, farleu being distinguished as the best good thing from ' heriot the best beast."

CHAPTER I.
Heriot Custom and Heriot Service.

HERIOT custom is that heriot which is due by virtue of an immemorial usage of a certain place or precinct, as within the Manor of Fairhurst. It is not due in respect of any particular parcel of land alienated or devised, but it is due on the death or alienation of *every* tenant of the manor. It is due on the death of A.B. not because he died seised of any particular close of land, but because at his death he was a tenant of the manor generally. It is due not by express reservation, but by reason of immemorial custom. Heriot service is due by reason of a particular and express *reservation* in the grant or lease, or is claimed by prescription, which presumes an original grant with such a reservation. According to Coke heriot custom lies in *prender* and not in *render*, it not being in the nature of a rent. Heriot service lies in *render*, being in the nature of a rent or founded in ancient tenure, and there would appear to be a preponderance of authority in favour of its lying in *prender* also. Lord Chief Justice Gilbert says that the heriot was a device first introduced to keep a conquered nation in subjection and to support the public strength and military furniture of the kingdom by taking on the death of the tenant his best armour. Hence it became part of the service arising from the tenure and therefore to be distrained for as other services, and when military service declined was turned into something of private profit to the lord and that instead of the *militiæ apparatus* he took the best horse, ox or cow, the same remedy [distress] being continued as when the heriot was paid in the habiliments of war.[1] The Chief Justice surmises that it being for the private safety of all the tenants of a manor that the habiliments of war should be kept among themselves for their defence, that therefore when there was no such tenure

---

[1] Gilb. Distresses, p. 9.

between the lord and tenants of some manor the tenants by agreement consented that the lord should have the best part of the military furniture, and that this agreement created a custom, which custom created a right in the lord to seize. But the lord could not distrain, because wherever there were any footsteps of a distress it was always supposed to be part of the feudal reservation; and the heriot custom arising originally from the grant of the tenant, and not being reserved by the lord upon his feudal donation, was not a service arising from the tenure between lord and tenant; and therefore was not under the regulation of feudal services and consequently not to be distrained for as such services were. But that where such heriot obtains, the property of the heriot is actually in the lord upon the death of the tenant; because the choice of the best beast is in the lord and not in the tenant. And that hence it is that the lord may seize the heriot custom wherever he finds it, either on the tenant's land or off it, or even in the king's highway, and that if it be removed [eloigned] he may have trespass or detinue for it, for the bringing the action determines the choice for the beast, as if he had seized it at first; and whoever takes it violates the property which was vested in the lord by the death of the tenant. But in the case of such eloignment the lord cannot distrain the tenant, as he may for the heriot service, because the distress was introduced for the recovery of the feudal duties of which the heriot custom is no part.

Heriot custom may be due on the death of every tenant of an estate of inheritance, or for life, or years,[1] or at will,[2] or upon the surrender or alienation of the tenant,[3] so by custom so much money may be due or the best chattel *loco heriotti* and not a beast,[4] and as the property in it vests immediately in the lord on the death of the tenant or on an alienation by him the lord may seize it in any place, though he cannot distrain for it.[5] Of course he cannot seize the beast of another.[6] But a seizure for

---

[1] 1 H. vii. 13 and 15; Keilw. 80; Bro. Hariot; 5 Kit. 133.
[2] 2 Buls. 196, *Hix* v. *Gardiner*.
[3] 3 H. vi. 45 b; Bro. Hariot, 8, Customes, 2; Kit. 134 b.
[4] Kit. 103 a (c).
[5] Keilw. 82 a, 84 b, 167 a; Bro. Hariot, 2, 6, 7; 1 Show. 81, *Parker* v. *Gage*; 1 Salk. 356, *Austin* v. *Bennett*.
[6] Cro. Car. 260, *Major* v. *Brandwood*.

heriot custom is not within the statute 11 Geo. ii. cap. 19, s. 22[1]; therefore in replevin as well as in trespass if the lord avows or justifies for heriot custom he ought to allege the seisin of himself, and the tenant, the custom for a heriot, the death of the tenant, and seizure of the heriot.[2] And it is not sufficient to allege a custom to take the best beast without saying *for a heriot or in the name of a heriot*.[3] And if the heriot be eloigned so that the lord cannot seize he may bring trover or detinue against him who detains it.[4]

It has long been doubted whether the lord might seize the heriot service, because that, being part of the feudal duties arising from the tenure between the lord and the tenant, ought to be governed by the same regulations with the other services: and therefore when a tenant holds by a capon or a hen, etc., the lord must distrain, and cannot seize as for his own property :— so neither ought he to seize for a heriot service, but it seems that the heriot service is seizable as well as the heriot custom; because the choice of the best beast is in the lord and therefore he only is to determine that choice by a seizure, but when the tenure is by the rent of a hen or a capon, etc., he is to render and therefore the lord can only compel him to do it by distress,[5] but a suit heriot reserved by deed cannot be taken off the manor.[6] It would appear, however, that if the heriot service be reserved upon a lease or by deed since the statute *Quia emptores* payable by a tenant in fee it is considered as a rent and can only be recovered like rent by distress, or action of debt, or covenant, but cannot be seized.[7] It seems clear that heriot service when part of the ancient tenure may be seized anywhere either in or out of the manor.[8] The lord may even seize it in the hands of a vendee unless the sale were in market overt, and unless (in the case of horses) all the requirements in the Acts of Philip

---

[1] 2 Wils. 28, *Lloyd* v. *Winton.*
[2] 2 Lutw. 1309, 10, *Baldwin* v. *Noakes.*
[3] Dy. 199 b ; see 1 Bosanq. and Pull. 282, *Parkin* v. *Radcliff.*
[4] Bro. Hariot, 6, 9 (d).
[5] Gilb. Distress.
[6] 1 Show. 81.
[7] 2 A. & E. 742, 743, per Cur.
[8] Plow. 96 a., *Woodland* v. *Mantel* ; Moor. 540, *Odiham* v. *Smith* ; Cro. Eliz. 589, *S. C.* ; Bro. Hariot, 2 ; 2 Lutw. 1367, *Osborne* v. *Sture* ; Fitzh. Hariot, 5 ; 1 Salk. 356, *Austin* v. *Bennett* ; 1 Show. 81, *Parker* v. *Guge* ; 3 Bac. Abr. 52. Willes, 192, *Edmunds* v. *Moseley.* Cro. Car. 260, *Major* v. *Brandwood*

and Mary, and of Elizabeth,[1] have been complied with. But no other than the tenant's own beast can be seized.[2] Thus where on a lease for three lives or ninety-nine years determinable on three lives there is reserved for a heriot upon the death of each life his or her best beast and the lease is assigned, and then one of the lives drops, the beast of the assignee cannot be seized, though the lessor may distrain upon the land for the best beast of the deceased tenant,[3] and the lord or lessor may *distrain* for a heriot *any man's* cattle that are upon the land without the lord's or lessor's default and retain them until the heriot is paid, or by stat. 2 W. & M. cap. 5 sell them if not replevied.[4] And therefore he cannot distrain for heriot service out of the manor or lands demised,[5] and if the tenant brings replevin the lord or lessor may avow generally under the stat. 11 Geo. ii. cap. 19, sec. 22, and it appears by the case of *Lanyon* v. *Carne*[6] in Charles the Second's time that an action of debt, or of covenant, lies to recover a heriot reserved upon a lease. In the case of a power to lease for lives so that the ancient rents and reservations are reserved, and the ancient lease has reserved as a heriot the best beast *of the lessee* (being one of the lives), *his executors, administrators or assigns, or such person as shall be in possession of the premises and entitled to the same by virtue of the lease*, it has been questioned whether a lease reserving only the best beast *of the tenant* (being one of the lives) is good. But a lease is not bad under such a power which reserves the best beast of the *person or persons who for the time being shall be tenant or tenants in possession of the premises*. Heriot service according to some of the ancient books was due only on the death of a tenant in fee, but as it is due by *reservation* it is manifest that it may be reserved on the grant of a less estate.[7]

---

1 2 and 3 P. & M. c. 7; 31 Eliz. c. 12.
2 Cro. Car. 260, *Major* v. *Brandwood*; Dig. 199 b, pl. 57; Ow. 146, S. P. per Anderson.
3 Rol. Abr. 451 (P); 2 Lutw. 1369.
4 Cro. Car. 260; Bro. Hariot, 6; 3 Mod. 231, *Osborne* v. *Steward.*
5 1 Salk. 356, *Austin* v. *Bennett.*
6 2 Saund. 165.
7 2 Saund. 165, *Lanyon* v. *Carne.*

CHAPTER II.

Of the different kinds of Heriots.

HERIOTS are divisible broadly into two classes—the best live beast and the best dead good. As the " best live beast " the most valuable racehorse of his time was actually seized for a heriot, and as the " best dead good " the Pitt Diamond and Rubens' famous picture, the " Chapeau de Paille," which is the gem of the Peel Collection in the National Gallery, were barely saved from seizure.[1] As different customs became established in different manors, it is customary in some manors to render to the lord the best animal of which the tenant died possessed, in others the second best beast ; in others the only beast if but one, or if the tenant has no beast then a fixed sum in lieu of a heriot[2] ; in others a fixed sum for a heriot,[3] while in some manors the custom is to render the best beast *or* good *or* a sum certain at the election of the lord ; and others are found in which the lord is entitled to the best beast if the tenant die possessed of a beast, otherwise the best dead good, or a sum certain. Where the heriot is the best chattel, a jewel, or piece of plate, may be claimed as a heriot.[4] From the Court Rolls themselves must be ascertained what the particular heriot in any particular manor may be. In some manors no heriots at all exist—in others heriots are due only from tenants of *some* of the lands held of the manor—this is heriot service as distinguished from heriot custom, the heriot due from *every* tenant of the manor. In an avowry for a heriot it is necessary to allege of what nature the heriot be, whether an animal or dead good.[5] When the tenant dies possessed of

---

[1] Sir Henry Maine's Early Law and Custom.
[2] Cowp. 62, *Griffen* v. *Blandford.*
[3] Kit. 103 a.
[4] Cru. Dig. IV. edit. vol. i. p. 304, s. 46.
[5] Hutt. 4, *Shaw* v. *Taylor*; 3 East, 260 ; 1 Bosanq. & Pull. 393, 4, *Purkin* v. *Radcliff.*

several animals it is to be ascertained by the lord which is the best, for he may take which he pleases as such, but if he do not seize the one which is the best—or even if he seize the worst— he must be content, and immediately on his election the property rests in him.[1] But if the tenant hold by rendering an ox as a heriot and the tenant have several oxen, the lord cannot make his choice, for the election is in the tenant, who may render which ox he will.[2] The lord is only entitled to the beast of his tenant, he cannot seize or prescribe to have the beast of a stranger.[3] The quality of the beast must be ascertained at the time of the tenant's death or alienation. If then the lord seize six months after the death or alienation he must seize, not the beast which may be the best at the end of the six months, but that which was the best on the day when the tenant died or aliened.[4] When the custom is that a beast *only* can be seized for a heriot—the custom not giving in default a dead good— then if at death or alienation the tenant have no beast the lord can have no heriot.[5] To prevent the lord's claim, the tenant before death or alienation frequently parted with his property in the beasts. The stat. 13 Eliz. cap. 5 was enacted with a view to remedy the evil, but as till death or alienation actually take place the lord can have no title to any beast or good of the tenant as a heriot, the property in the chattels of the tenant being undoubtedly in himself, it is manifest that the tenant has a right to dispose of them as he pleases, unless the alienation be " contrived of malice, fraud, covin, collusion, or guile to the end, purpose, and intent to delay, hinder, or defraud the lord of his heriot." And as fraud shall never be intended or pre-sumed, such disposition must be proved to have been made to the end and for the purpose of defrauding the lord of his heriot, or the lord or person alleging such fraud cannot avail himself

---

[1] Hil. 16 Hen. vii. pl. 3. fol. 4—5 ; Hob. 60 and Bro. Har. pl. 11 ; Cro. Eliz. 589, *Odiham v. Smith*.

[2] Cro. Eliz. 589, *Odiham v. Smith*.

[3] Dy. 199 b, *Purton v. Mason and Marg.* (58) ; Cro. Eliz. 725, *Parker v. Combleford* ; Moor. 16, *Wilson v. Wise*.

[4] Bro. Hariot 8 ; Kit. 135 b, 136 a ; Hut. 4—5, *Shaw v. Taylor* ; Mich. 6 Edw. iii. pl. 3, fol. 36 a ; Plow. Queries, Q. 64 ; Wat. Cop. Tit. Heriots.

[5] Keilw. 84 b ; Hut. 4, *Shaw* v. *Taylor* ; Carter, 86 ; 4 Leon. 239, pl. 377 ; 2 Black. Comm. 424.

of the statute.[1]   The tenant cannot defeat the lord's claim by will, the lord's title is preferred to that of the legatee.[2]

---

[1] 2 Brownl. 187, *Tyrer* v. *Littleton*, 10 Co. 56 a, *S.C.* cited.
[2] Co. Litt. 185 b.

CHAPTER III.

Persons from whom Heriots are Due.

HERIOT Custom can only be due on the death or alienation of a tenant.[1] Heriot Service reserved on a particular grant or lease, being merely the agreement of the contracting parties, may be reserved on the happening of any particular event. A custom for a heriot on the death of any person dying within the manor, or on that of a stranger, cannot be supported.[2] On the death of a *tenant* a heriot (whether heriot custom or heriot service) may be claimed and that whether such tenant held in fee,[3] for life,[4] for years,[5] or at will only.[6] It is not, however, necessary that such tenant be *the tenant paravail*, for a person having the *mesnalty* may equally hold by heriot.[7] If A. disseise B. yet B. will continue tenant to the lord by right and a heriot will be due not on the death of the disseisor, but of the disseisee.[8] In the case of a surrender passed and death of the surrenderor before admission of the surrenderee a heriot becomes due on the death of such surrenderor as at the time of his death he was tenant to the lord.[9]

Joints Tenants being seised *per mie et per tout*, the heriot is not due until the last life drops.[10]

Coparceners are like joint tenants seised *per mie et per tout*,[11] and no heriot is due so long as one of them survive.

---

[1] 2 Roll. Abr. 518, Tenure (H).
[2] Cro. Eliz. 725, *Parker v. Combleford*.
[3] Bro. Har. 5.
[4] Bro. Har. 5; Kit. 133 a; 2 Saund. 165, *Lanyon v. Carne*; 3 Salk. 181, *Osborne v. Sture*.
[5] Kit. 133 a, *Lanyon v. Carne, vide supra*.
[6] 2 Buls. 196 in *Hix v. Gardiner*.
[7] 2 Saund. 165, *Lanyon v. Carne;* Wat. Cop. ii. page 156.
[8] 2 Roll. Abr. 72 (year 1668 edit.); Wat. Cop. ii. page 156.
[9] Wat. Cop. vol. i.
[10] Mich. 24 Edw. iii. pl. 88, fol. 72 b; Bro. Har. 4; Fitzh. Har. 3 & 5, præscript 29; Kit. 134 a & b; Ow. 152, *Butler v. Archer*.
[11] Lib. Assisa. 210 b, Edw. iii. pl. 15.

Tenants in Common having several estates and each being solely seised, a heriot is due on the death of each, but if the several shares become reunited in one person, thenceforth only one heriot is due.[1]

The Reversioner's death yields a heriot.[2]

Particular Tenant and Remainderman. A copyholder for life in a manor where the custom was that if the tenant died seised a heriot should be paid, was disseised and died; the lord having first granted the seigniory to A. for 99 years if the tenant should so long live, remainder to B. for 1000 years. Two questions were made, first whether any heriot should be paid because the copyholder did not die seised—as to this the court held clearly that a heriot was due and payable, for notwithstanding the ouster and disseisin the copyholder still continued legal tenant, and such disseisin might have been by combination to defeat the lord of his heriot. Second to whom the heriot should be paid—as to this the court held clearly that the remainderman for 1000 years could have no right to it because the copyholder was not his tenant, and as to the grantee for 99 years it was doubted, because the moment the copyholder died his estate was determined.[3]

A heriot is not due on the death of a person having an *interesse termini*.[4]

Cestui que Trust's death gives no heriot, but it is due on the death of the trustee who is tenant to the lord.[5]

Feme Covert. It has always hitherto been held that on the death of a feme covert the lord can have no heriot on the ground that she can (as such) have no personal chattels.[6] But this reasoning will not apply in cases where she has a separate estate[7] and since the Married Woman's Property Acts it is

---

1 2 Bing. 272, *Garland* v. *Jekyll*, overruling 6 East, 481, *Attree* v. *Scutt*, and see J. Bayley's Judgt. in *Holloway* v. *Berkley*, 6 Barn. & Cres. page 3.

2 Pasch. 44 Edw. iii. pl. 13a, fol. 24; Bro. Avowrie 142; Ow. 152, *Butler* v. *Archer*.

3 Cru. Dig. vol. i. p. 304; Mar. 23, *Norris* v. *Norris*; 2 Roll. Abr. 72, 1668 edit.

4 2 Keb. 505, *Lemal* v. *Cara*.

5 1 Vern. 441, *Trin. Coll. Cam.* v. *Browne*.

6 Keilw. 84 a & b; 4 Leon. 239, Ca. 377.

7 Wat. Cop. ii. p. 162, note (t).

apprehended that a heriot may be claimed on the death of a feme covert if she die possessed of any personal property.

Husband. If the husband of a tenant die in her lifetime no heriot is due on his death. The husband and wife are seised by entireties and on the husband's death the seisin remains in the wife.[1]

Wife. If the wife predecease the husband, and the custom of the manor gives the husband his courtesy either in part of or in the whole estate a heriot will be due on his death, for he is in by the act of the law and is tenant to the lord.[2]

Dowress. First as to customary freeholds. The widow (except when she takes the whole estate) is tenant to the heir. No heriot is due therefore on her death unless by the custom of the manor her free-bench extends to the whole estate.[3] Secondly as to copyholds. The widow is tenant to the lord whether she take the whole or a portion only of the lands[4] and therefore a heriot must be due on her death. Whatever portion she takes, it is called her free-bench, which implies that she becomes a bencher. If she has a right to sit as a bencher, or on the homage, she must be tenant to the lord, for none but tenants to the lord have a right to sit in such capacity in the lord's court.[5] A widow taking a portion of the copyhold as her free-bench, or the husband as his courtesy, takes not a common law, but a copyhold interest, and therefore must hold that interest by copy of court roll of the lord and must be a tenant to the lord, and therefore a heriot is due on his or her death.[6] But it seems that if the customary heir or the husband entitled to courtesy in the copyhold of his wife or the wife entitled to free-bench in the copyhold of her husband—where the lord could compel admission to such courtesy or free-bench—should die without being admitted, no heriot would be due.[7]

Corporation. In the event of a Corporation owning heriotable land, it is said that by special custom a heriot may be due

---

1 Dougl. 329, *Polyblank v. Hawkins.*   •
2 2 Inst. 301.
3 Wat. Cop. ii. p. 147.
4 Gilb. Ten. 172, 3 ; 2 Show. 184, *Chapman v. Sharpe.*
5 Wat. Cop. ii. page 164, note (e).
6 Wat. Cop. ii. p. 165.
7 Mo. 272 in *Ever v. Aston* ; Scriv. by Brown, p. 219.

on the death or avoidance of its head.[1]

Several Tenements. When a person possesses several tenements held of the same manor, all of which are heriotable, a heriot upon his death is due in respect of each tenement[2] unless there be a custom in the manor to the contrary. Such a custom is said to have been disallowed in Chancery 12 June, 1615.[3]

A heriot may be due on the alienation of the tenancy as well as on the death of the tenant. But to support this a special custom or an express or presumed reservation must be proved.[4] It has already been stated [*ante* page 13] that a heriot claimed as being due from an *incoming* tenant has not been held to be a bad custom. It appears that a heriot is due (where the custom gives it on an alienation) on the surrender of a particular copyhold interest however small, but that no heriot is due on the grant of a particular interest by a customary freeholder. It also seems that a heriot will be due on the alienation of a reversion equally with that of an estate in possession.[5] Having now dealt with the alienation of part of the *estate* or *interest* in heriotable lands, we pass on to the consideration of the alienation of part of the *lands* themselves. Before doing so we may remark that when a husband is seised of a manor in right of his wife it is essential to the validity or a grant of copyhold that it should be made in both their names, and the husband therefore could not proceed by seizure of distress for the recovery of a heriot in his own name only, but if put to avow must make title through his wife and those under whom she claims, and then allege the marriage, and that the entry and seizure or distress were made by the husband and wife in her right, and so justify.[6]

---

[1] Long Quinto, Mich. 5 Edw. iv. fol. 72 b; Fitzh. Hariot, 7; Trin. 1. Edw. ii. 2, 14 a.

[2] Kit. 134 a; 6 Co. 1, *Bruerton's case*; Wat. Cop. ii. 166.

[3] 13 Jac. Decree, *Ld. Gerrard*, complainant, and *Abnett and others*, defts., as to the Manor of Audley. See Godb. 265, *Lord Gerrard's case*.

[4] Kit. 133 a & b, 134, 135; Wat. Cop. ii. page 167.

[5] Wat. Cop. ii. pp. 168, 9.

[6] "Cases and Opinions," pubd. 1791, 216, 217. Scriv. by Brown, 223.

CHAPTER IV.

Multiplication of Heriots.

IT appears to be on all hands agreed that on the alienation of part of the lands the heriot shall be multiplied. For if A. be seised of forty acres of land, and he alien ten acres to B., and ten acres to C., and ten acres to D., and retain the other ten himself, the lord shall have four heriots, *i.e.*, one on the alienation to B., one on that to C., a third on that to D., and a fourth on A.'s alienation of the remaining ten acres.[1] It was formerly held that even if A. afterwards repurchased the lands from B., C., and D., the four heriots would continue to be payable.[2] But since the decision in *Garland* v. *Jekyll*,[3] and *Holloway and others* v. *Berkeley*,[4] and having regard to the case of *Abingdon* v. *Lipscombe*,[5] it would appear doubtful whether such a contention can any longer be supported. There must manifestly be *some* limit to the multiplication; Chief Justice Best in his judgement in *Garland* v. *Jekyll* said "The claim of the lord must not be carried to such an extent as would work the disherison of the copyholder.........an undue multiplication of heriots would make his estate what the civilians call *damnosa hæreditas*." The cases of *Garland* v. *Jekyll*, and *Holloway* v. *Berkeley*, left it still unsettled whether in a case where there had been an actual severance and division of a tenement into distinct and separate parcels so as to give to separate holders separate properties in severalty the multiplication of heriots after a reunion of the same land in one person continued, for in this respect *Attree* v. *Scutt* and *Garland* v. *Jekyll* are at variance, and in the subsequent

---

[1] Fitzh. Har. pl. 1; Kit. 134 a, 135 b; 6 Co. 1, *Bruerton's case*; 8 Co. 104 b, *Talbot's case*; 2 Brownl. 293, *Chapman* v. *Pendleton*; 2 Roll. Abr. 514, Ten. Wat. Cop. ii. page 170.

[2] Fitzh. Har. pl. 1. 8 Co. 105 a; Wat. Cop. ii. page 171; 6 East. 476, *Attree* v. *Scutt*.

[3] 2 Bing. 272.

[4] 6 Barn. & Cres. page 3.

[5] 1 Gale & Dav. 230.

case of *Holloway* v. *Berkeley* the court expressing their opinion that the matter was still open for argument abstained from saying anything on the point. But in the case of *Abingdon* v. *Lipscombe* it appears to have been conceded that the multiplication did not continue after the reunion.

In *Attree* v. *Scutt* Lord Ellenborough in his judgement said, "It has been settled so long ago as the time of Edward the Third that if my tenant, who holds of me by a heriot, alien parcel of the land to another, each of them is chargeable to me with a heriot, for it is entire; and if the tenant purchase the land again, yet if I were seised of the heriot by another man I shall have of him the tenant *for each portion* a heriot. This doctrine is to be found in Fitzh. Abr. tit. Heriot, pl. 1, and from thence it follows that if an estate holden by indivisible services be divided and holden in severalty, and afterwards by the act of the parties shall come again into one hand, the services which were multiplied shall continue to be payable, not as for one tenement, but for *each portion* respectively, *i.e.*, as for distinct tenements, and that they do not again become in respect of the lord one tenement." The decision in *Attree* v. *Scutt* appears to have depended entirely on the authority of the passage in Fitzherbert. In *Garland v. Jekyll* it was decided that a copyhold property, which when in the hands of a single owner pays but one heriot, but pays more if divided among several owners as *tenants in common*, shall again pay but one heriot if it again becomes united in the person of single owner, but in that case there was no actual severance and division of the tenement into distinct and separate parcels. Chief Justice Best gave it as his opinion that no deference was due to the authority of the case in Fitzherbert, and that it was quite clear that the noble and learned judge did not look at the case to which Fitzherbert referred for his authority, for that if he had he would have found that there was no such case. The Chief Justice in his judgement said "Let us see if there is any deference due to the authority of the case in Fitzherbert. To avoid any mistake I have copied it in the Norman French, which I translate thus: 'If my tenant who holds from me aliene parcels of his land to others, every one of them will owe to me an heriot because the heriot is entire; and if the same tenant purchases back again I shall have two heriots from him.' And Fitzherbert says that

was the opinion of Wyl. and Shard.   Fitzherbert does not mean
to refer to the year books as Lord Ellenborough supposes, for
when he does he not only mentions the term and the year of the
reign as ' Hilary 34 Edw. ill.,' but he puts a figure to denote the
number of the case in the year book.   Here then is no figure.
It is certainly not in the year books that have come down to us,
for looking at the year books of Edw. iii. they stop at the 30th
Edw. iii., and they do not begin again till the 38th, so that there
is no year book for the 34 Edw. iii.   The next thing I have to
advert to destroys the case altogether, it is that there were no
judges living in the 34 Edw. iii. whose names answer to Wyl.
and Shard.   It is clear therefore that there is some great mistake
as to that case.   It was a loose note, probably the decision
of a judge at *Nisi Prius*.   It will not be found in any one book
of authority, for if so we should have found it in Brooke, Rolle's
Abridgement, Viner or Comyns.   Fitzherbert's Abridgement is
the compilation of a learned judge, but even learned judges may
sometimes make mistakes.   And the authority on which the
case of *Attree* v. *Scutt* depends has crept into Fitzherbert and
is not supported by any other authority.   We see the only
ground on which the case of *Attree* v. *Scutt* rests and we find it
cannot be supported.   We find that if the learned judges had
endeavoured to trace the case in Fitzherbert to its source they
would have seen it had no solid foundation.   There is nothing
on which it can stand and therefore we have no difficulty in
deciding against it."

In the case of *Holloway* v. *Berkeley*, a case relating to the
Manor of Bosham in Sussex, *Garland* v. *Jekyll* was followed,
and it was decided that when a copyhold tenement holden by
heriot custom becomes the property of several as tenants in
common, the lord is entitled to a heriot from each of them ; but
that if the several portions be re-united in one person one
heriot only is payable.

Bayley, J., in the course of his judgement said, "The
question in this case was whether double heriots were payable
upon in respect of what had heretofore been six copyhold
tenements.   They were held of the Manor of Bosham, and by
the custom of that manor there is payable to the lord on the
death of any tenant of any of the copyhold tenements called
Boardland dying seised thereof, as and for a heriot in respect of

each of the six copyhold tenements the tenant's best beast.   In
April 1812 John Andrews died seised of these tenements,
having previously surrendered them to the use of his will and
having devised them to his two sons, George Hazelar Andrews
and James Andrews, as tenants in common in fee.   In August
1812 the two brothers were respectively admitted to undivided
moieties, and in February 1818 James surrendered his moiety to
his brother George Hazelar, and he was admitted thereto·
There never therefore was any dying seised whilst the moieties
were in different ownerships, no heriot ever payable for a
separate moiety, and no instance in which the heriots were in
fact multiplied.   In 1824 G. H. Andrews died seised and upon
his death the lord seized two beasts in respect of each of the
six copyholds, and for the seizure of six, *i.e.*, all but one on
each, this action was brought.   The question therefore in sub-
stance is whether upon a tenancy in common the share of each
tenement constitutes *a distinct tenement*, or whether, notwithstanding the distinct *estates* of each tenant in common, the
copyhold does not still remain an entire tenement.   The custom
(which is against common right and to be construed strictly)
gives a heriot in respect of each *tenement* of which the copyholder dies seised.   It is not in respect of *each estate* in a
copyhold tenement of which the tenant dies seised, but in
respect of each *tenement*.   In the case of heriot service or heriot
custom the law multiplies the heriot in two cases, one where
the tenement is actually divided and *converted into two or more*
separate tenements, the other when the tenement is left entire,
but different persons have distinct undivided estates therein.
Before the statute of *Quia emptores*, if tenant in fee who held
under certain services aliened part of his land in fee without the
lord's assent the lord might nevertheless distrain either upon the
land sold or upon the land retained for the whole of his services,
and the lord was entitled to consider the whole tenement as if
it remained entire, [10 H. 7, 10, pl. 26, Co. Litt. 43 a], and because
this statute did not bind the king, the same continued in the
king's case notwithstanding this statute, [Plowden, 240].   But in
ordinary cases since the statute any *freehold* tenant may subdivide his tenement, and alien part, and such of his services as
are divisible will be liable to be apportioned, and such of his
services as are entire will be multiplied, but the alienee will in

such case hold his portion as an entire independent tenement, his portion will be liable to the apportioned proportion only of the divisible services, and the residue will also be held as an entire independent tenement liable only to its apportioned proportion of the divisible services. If for instance C. has 300 acres of freehold land held at £15 rent, fealty, homage, and heriot, and he alien 100 acres to A., 100 to B., and retains 100 to himself, and each hundred acres is of the same value, A. will hold 100 acres at £5 rent, fealty, homage, and heriot, and B. and C. respectively will do the same, and each will hold his proportion as a separate independent tenement. A.'s tenement and B.'s and C.'s respectively will no longer be liable to the £15 rent, but to the £5 only, and it is not necessary in this case to say whether by the union of the three tenements in one person the £15 rent would again be revived and extend over the whole estate, or whether the three tenements would each continue a distinct tenement liable to its £5 only. If a copyhold tenant can subdivide his tenement in the same manner, the same consequences follow. But will the creation of a tenancy in common have the same effect in producing even for a time separate tenements ? Where the tenement is subdivided each tenant holds his share in severalty, and it is subject to nothing beyond its own services. In the case of a tenancy in common the tenement is undivided, none of the tenents in common, be there what number there may, knows his own in severalty; the services which in case of division would be divisible remain entire, and the whole land is subject to all the services. In case of copyholds they are not within the statutes of Partition, because the *alteration of the tenure*, without the lord's consent, may sound to the lord's prejudice, [Co. Cop. sec. 54, *Rowden* v. *Maltster*, Cro. Car. 44, Com. Dig. Copy. O]. And how will the tenure be altered but by splitting into two or more several tenements what was before an entire tenement ? In the comment upon the second chapter of the statute of *Quia emptores* Lord Coke makes the distinction between the alienee of the distinct parcel of a freehold tenement and the creation of a tenancy in common. That branch of the statute provides 'that if a freeman sell any part of his lands or tenements, the feoffee shall hold immediately of the chief lord, and shall be forthwith charged with the services for so much as belongs or ought to belong to the chief lord for that parcel [*particula illa*] according to the quantity of the land or tenement so sold. And so in this case the same part of the services shall remain to the chief lord to be taken by the hands of the feoffee, for the which he ought to be attendant upon and answerable to the chief lord according to the quantity of land or tenement sold for the parcel of the services so due.' This provision is the foundation of apportionment in these cases; rent, where that is one of services, not being apportionable at Common Law. Upon that part of this claim which relates to the holding part of the chief lord, and at a proportion of the service, Lord Coke's Commentary [2 Inst. 503] is this: '*particula illa*, for which he is to be charged, is understood of a part *in severalty*, and not in common, and therefore it is holden that if the tenant make a feoffment in fee of the moiety or third part of the tenancy that such a feoffee is not within the purview of this statute; for a moiety or third part *pro indiviso* is not *particula*, for that part implieth a part in severalty' [6 Co. 1 b]. And the meaning of this passage is very distinctly explained in Bro. Abr. Tenures, pl. 64, from 29 Hen. viii., which Lord Coke cites. 'A man makes feoffment of the moiety of his land; the feoffee shall hold of the lord by the entire services by which the entire land was held before, for the statute *tenendo pro particulâ* has not place here, for a moiety is not *particula* and there is a contrariety between one or two acres in certain and a third part, or the like, which extends through the part and the whole (*q. va. per mye et per tout*).' This authority therefore shows clearly that in the case of freehold lands which are within the statute of *Quia emptores* the creation of a tenancy in common leaves the services entire, and, consequently must leave the tenement entire also; and if this be the case in freeholds, *à fortiori* must it be in the case of copyholds. Coke's Copyholder, s. 56, page 130, is an authority in the case of copyholds upon the same point; for after noticing that 'if several copyholds join in a grant of their copyholds by one copy, or if one copyholder having several copyholds grants them by one copy, yet the grantee shall pay several fines, for they shall enure as several grants,' he adds, 'but if two joint tenants, two tenants in common, or tenant for life and he in remainder, join in the grant of a copyhold, one fine only is due and it shall enure as one grant only.' Kitchen, 245, is nearly to the same

purpose: ' Also if tenant for life and he in remainder or reversion join in a surrender to one and to heirs, he to whose use the surrender is made shall pay but one fine, for it is but one admittance and not several, and one surrender and not several, and there is but one tenant admitted; the same law where two joint tenants, two tenants in common or coparceners surrender to one and his heirs shall be paid but one fine.' These authorities appear to me to establish a plain distinction between the alienation of an entire part and the creation of a tenancy in common, and to shew that though the former may split one tenement into several the latter will not. I would notice also that the former, the alienation of an entire part, must always be the act of the owner in fee of the whole, so that whoever feels the consequences must claim through the person by whose act they were occasioned; whereas the owner of a part of the tenement only, viz.: one of several joint tenants, or one of several parceners may create a tenancy in common, and if a tenancy in common would create a division into distinct tenements every division would increase the number of tenements in geometrical progression. Dividing the whole *six times* into moieties (which would be allowing something short of one division every century since the commencement of legal memory) would make what was originally one tenement 64 (2—4—8—16—32—64) and dividing it six times into three shares would make it 729 (3—9—27—81—243—729) and we might have in pleading—what I apprehend has never yet been seen—a statement that a man was seised in his demesne as of fee at the will of the lord according to the custom of the manor of 729 undivided parts of certain copyhold lands, the whole into 729 parts to be divided. Such a singularity will I trust never be seen; but whatever may at any time have been the number of tenants in common of what was originally one copyhold tenement, when all the interests are again vested in one person, he may consider himself as seised, not of so many undivided portions of the land, but as the sole proprietor of one entire estate and tenement. And if this be the true view of the effect of a tenancy in common, and the proper light in which the question in this case ought to be viewed, it will not be necessary to occupy much time in noticing the authorities which were relied upon in the argument. The authority from Fitzherbert is the case not of the creation of a tenancy in common, but of a severance of the estate into distinct *parcels*, and the alienation of one of those parcels of his land to others. And if we are right in supposing that the creation of a tenancy in common, in what was previously an entire tenement, will not destroy the entirety of the tenement, it is immaterial to consider what will be the effect of severing a tenement into distinct parcels. It does not appear from Fitz-herbert whether that was the case of a *copyhold* or of a *freehold* tenement, but it has been frequently noticed in subsequent cases, and it is a relief to us not to be called upon to impeach it. Whether it be a right or a wrong decision we consider a matter still open for discussion. In *Attree* v. *Scutt* it may be difficult to collect from the Reports whether there was not a severance of the tenements, so as to allot to one tenement what had previously been parcel of another ; but the judgement of the Court appears to have proceeded upon the ground that the creation of a tenancy in common, though there was no division or severance of the property, created distinct and separate tenements, and in that respect we think that decision wrong ; *Garland* v. *Jckyll* was a case of the creation of a tenancy in common, and upon the principle that the creation of a tenancy in common leaves the tenement entire we think the decision in that case right. It is not necessary for us to say what would have been our opinion had that been a case in which there had been an actual severance and division of a tenement into distinct and separate parcels, so as to have given to separate holders separate properties in severalty, and we cautiously abstain from saying anything on that point."

CHAPTER V.

Extinction of Heriots.

UNITY of possession by the lord of the land who ought to have heriot by custom is an extinguishment of the heriot custom, for it is a custom that *runs with the Seigniory*, contrary of a custom that runs with the land as Gavelkind, Borough English, and such like.[1]

There is a difference between heriot custom and heriot service as to the extinguishment thereof by the lord purchasing part of the tenancy; for by such means the heriot service is extinct, but if the custom of the manor be, that upon the death of every tenant of the manor dying seised of any land held of the same manor the lord shall have a heriot, then though the lord purchase part of the tenancy yet he shall have a heriot by the custom of the manor for the residue, for he remains tenant to the lord and the custom extends to every tenant.[2] "Comment que le Seignior purchase parcel de la terre uncore il avera heriot par le residue car ces est entier et nient annuel."[3] It appears in the case of lands subject to heriot custom escheating to the lord, or in any other way becoming vested in him, that if the lord after such escheat or vesting regrant the lands they would still be subject to heriot custom,[4] but if the lands regranted be customary freehold lands, no heriot can possibly be claimed by the lord of the manor afterwards, for by the regrant in fee the lands would be immediately separated from and no longer held of that manor by the custom of which the heriot is claimed, as they would be held of lord above. If there be lord and tenant by fealty and heriot service and the tenant aliens part of the tenancy the alienee shall hold by a

---

1 Vin. Abr. Tit. Herriot, H.
2 8 Rep. 10 b, Trin. 7 Jac. i.—the fourth resolution in *Talbot's case*, Vin. Abr. Tit. Heriot.
3 8 Coke, 106.
4 Kit. 134 b, *Talbot's case*, and *Chapman* v. *Pendleton*; Wat. Cop. ii. page 171.

distinct heriot service. And if after the alienation the lord
purchase the residue of the tenancy, only the heriot service due
from the first tenant shall be extinguished, because by the
alienation each held his proportion by a separate and distinct
tenure, and therefore, if the lord purchase one tenancy, that can
no way affect the services of his other tenants, but if the lord,
before the tenancy had been separated and held by two distinct
tenures, purchased part of it, the whole heriot service had been
extinct.[1]

Heriot custom is not within the Statute of Limitation.[2]
To an action of trespass for seizing and taking a horse the
defendant pleaded an immemorial custom for the lord of the
manor upon the death of a free tenant to seize the best beast
of which the tenant died possessed wherever it could be found,
and that in 1873 on the death of a tenant the defendant as lord
of the manor took the horse under this custom. Replication
that more than twenty years before the heriot in question
became due, a heriot became due, for which the then lord of
the manor, through whom the defendant claimed, did not seize
though he could have done so; that the then lord, whilst
entitled, discontinued the taking of heriots; that no heriot had
since been taken until the trespass complained of; that the
right to make an entry, or distress, or bring an action to recover
heriots, at the time of such discontinuance then first accrued
to the then lord within 3 & 4 Wm. iv. cap. 27; and that such
right so first accrued more than twenty years before the death
of the tenant or the trespass complained of—on demurrer:—
Held that the replication was bad since the seizure by the
defendant was not making an entry or distress, nor bringing an
action to recover rent within the meaning of the said statute,
and that the defendant's title to heriots therefore was not
barred by the lapse of twenty years. *Quære* whether, notwithstanding the interpretation of "rent" in section 1, heriot
service and heriot custom or either of them are within the
enactments of sections 2, 3, 34 and 42.[3]

---

1 Gilb. on Rents, 171.
2 Stat. 3 & 4 Wm. iv. cap 27, ss. 1, 2, 3, 34, 42.
3 *Lord Zouche* v. *Dalbiac*, L.R., X. Exch. 172.

CHAPTER VI.

Enfranchisement of Heriots.

THE 27th section of the Copyhold Act, 1852, [15 & 16 Vic. cap. 51] gave power to enfranchise freehold or customary freehold lands holden of any manor from heriots. This section was repealed by the Act of 1858 [21 & 22 Vic. cap. 94]. But similar provisions as to heriots were made by section seven of that Act. This seventh section has in its turn been repealed by the fifty-first section of the Copyhold Act of 1887 [50 & 51 Vic. c. 73] and this last Act alone now gives the power of compulsory enfranchisement from heriots. The sections in the Act, so far as they relate to such enfranchisement, are given *in extenso*.

Sec. VII.   Subject to the provisions of the 48th section of the Copyhold Act, 1852, and to the provisions hereinbefore expressed, any lord, or tenant, or owner of any land liable to any heriot, or to any quit-rent, free-rent, or other manorial incident whatsoever may require and compel the extinguishment of such rights or incidents and the release and enfranchisement of the land subject thereto, and the same proceedings shall thereupon be had as are in the Copyhold Acts mentioned with reference to the enfranchisement of copyhold land, or as near thereto as the nature of the case will admit. [The " provisions hereinbefore expressed " appear to refer to section 4, by which it is provided that on every enfranchisement after the passing of the Act the lord of the manor shall continue to be entitled in case of escheat for want of heirs to the same right and interest in the land as he would have had if it had not been enfranchised].

Sec. IX.   The sixth section of the Copyhold Act, 1858, shall be amended as follows:—instead of the words " admittance or death " shall be read the words " admittance or enrolment on alienation "; and instead of the final word " heriot " shall be read the word " enrolment."

Sec. X. Section 8 of the Copyhold Act 1858 shall be read as if the word "thirty" had been inserted therein for "twenty" [and subject to certain other modifications in no way affecting the subject of heriots].

Sec. XI. The valuers appointed under the provisions of the Copyhold Acts shall determine the value of the manorial and other rights and incidents, such value to be a gross sum of money, and their decision shall be in such form as the Commissioners shall prescribe, and they shall in every case deliver the details of the valuation to the Commissioners, and if it shall appear to the Commissioners that the valuation is imperfect or erroneous they may remit it for reconsideration or correction; and if the valuers neglect or refuse to amend the same, the Commissioners may, after due notice to the lord and to the tenant, and after fully considering all the circumstances brought before them, determine the value of the manorial and other rights and incidents at such a sum as they may deem just and reasonable.

Sec. XXX. The Land Commissioners shall frame and cause to be printed and published such a scale of compensation for the enfranchisement of land from the manorial and other rights and incidents specified or referred to in the Copyhold Acts, including heriots, as in their judgement will be fair and just and will facilitate enfranchisement, and such scale shall contain all such directions for the guidance of lord, tenant, and valuers as the Commissioners may deem necessary. The said Commissioners shall also print and publish a scale of allowance to valuers for services to be performed in the execution of the Copyhold Acts. The Commissioners may from time to time vary any such scales, which are to be for guidance only, and not to be binding as a matter of law in any particular case, but the party requiring enfranchisement shall state to the other party whether or no he is willing to adopt the scale.

Sec. XXXI. If pending any proceedings commenced after the passing of this Act for enfranchisement under the Copyhold Acts the lord or tenant shall die, there shall be no abatement of the proceedings; any fresh admittance or enrolment consequent on such death and pending such proceedings shall be made without the payment of any fine, relief, or heriot to the lord; and the enfranchisement shall be proceeded with and the com-

pensation shall be ascertained on the same footing as if the enfranchisement had been effected immediately after the commencement of such proceedings.

The fifty-first section repeals [*inter alia*] the seventh section of the Act of 1852 and the same section of the Act of 1858.

In accordance with section 30 of the Act of 1887 the Land Commissioners have framed and published [under date of February, 1888] a " Scale of Compensation in ordinary cases of Enfranchisement of Copyholds of Inheritance." The paragraphs in such scale applying to heriots are Nos. 7, 8, 9 and 10. They are as follows :—

7. The compensation for a heriot payable on alienation by, as well as on the death of, a tenant, may be calculated by multiplying the value of the heriot by one half of the number of years' purchase given in the table [*post* p. 41] according to the age of the tenant.

8. The value of a heriot may generally be ascertained from the average value of the last three heriots taken or paid in respect of the property to be enfranchised. If that information cannot be obtained, or will not apply, the following circumstances should be taken into consideration in fixing the value of a heriot ; namely, the nature of the heriot, the character and value of the property, the condition in life of the tenant, and also whether the heriot can be seized as well without as within the manor.

9. The table being calculated on the assumption that fines and heriots are payable both on alienation by, and on the death of, a tenant, when a fine, whether arbitrary or certain, or a heriot, is payable only on one of those events, then only one half of the compensation calculated as previously directed should be given.

10. In manors in which fines or heriots are payable on the death of the lord, as well as on alienation by, or on the death of, a tenant, the compensation on enfranchisement should be increased according to the nature and amount of the customary fine or heriot payable in the manor on the death of the lord.

It should be borne in mind that the scale is for guidance only *and is not binding as a matter of law*, but the party requiring enfranchisement should in accordance with the Act state to the other party whether or no he is willing to adopt the scale.

Where a tenant was admitted before the 1st of July, 1853, he cannot compel enfranchisement until after payment or tender of the value of such a heriot as would be payable on admittance or alienation subsequent to the 1st of July, 1853.

Table referred to in the Scale of Compensation for Enfranchisement
issued by the Land Commissioners 1888.

Age of Tenant.	No. of Years' Purchase.	Age of Tenant.	No. of Years' Purchase.	Age of Tenant.	No. of Years' Purchase.
5 or under	2.29	37	3.26	70	4.50
		38	3.29	71	4.54
6	2.32	39	3.33	72	4.57
7	2.34	40	3.36	73	4.60
8	2.37	41	3.40	74	4.63
9	2.40	42	3.43	75	4.67
10	2.43	43	3.46	76	4.70
11	2.46	44	3.50	77	4.73
12	2.49	45	3.53	78	4.76
13	2.52	46	3.57	79	4.78
14	2.55	47	3.60	80	4.81
15	2.58	48	3.64	81	4.83
16	2.61	49	3.67	82	4.85
17	2.63	50	3.71	83	4.88
18	2.66	51	3.75	84	4.90
19	2.69	52	3.78	85	4.92
20	2.73	53	3.82	86	4.94
21	2.76	54	3.86	87	4.95
22	2.79	55	3.90	88	4.97
23	2.82	56	3.93	89	4.99
24	2.85	57	3.97	90	5.00
25	2.88	58	4.01	91	5.02
26	2.91	59	4.06	92	5.03
27	2.94	60	4.10	93	5.05
28	2.97	61	4.14	94	5.06
29	3.00	62	4.18	95	5.08
30	3.04	63	4.23	96	5.10
31	3.07	64	4.27	97	5.12
32	3.10	65	4.31	98	5.13
33	3.13	66	4.35	99	5.15
34	3.16	67	4.39	100 or upwards	5.16
35	3.20	68	4.43		
36	3.23	69	4.47		

INDEX.

A

ℱ

ℌ

Q

R

S

T

U

W

www.ingramcontent.com/pod-product-compliance
Lightning Source LLC
Chambersburg PA
CBHW020310090426
42735CB00009B/1300